Red Pill Prophet

The Secret of Déjà vu

BRANT FRICKER

DEDICATION

This book is dedicated to my brilliant, beautiful and incredibly talented wife Kristy who has loved me unconditionally and has shared many adventures with me, to my mother Sherrie who raised me to believe there was nothing I couldn't do as she pinned on my superman towel cape each morning as a boy, to my Pop David Todd who modeled true masculinity and wisdom during my most formidable years, and to the rest of my family and friends who have always encouraged me to live a fearless life of destiny. Most of all I dedicate this book to my King and old friend, The Ancient of Days, You amaze me every day with your love and unspeakable joy, I'm forever grateful.

CONTENTS

ACKNOWLEDGEMENTS

Thank you, Katherine Morris for your editing, Meri Brock for your coordination, Kristy Fricker for your proofing, Ron Garverick for your publishing advice and David Munoz for your brilliant graphic design.

INTRODUCTION

1101001 1101110 1110100 1110010 1101111 1100100 1110101 1100011
1110100 1101001 1101111 1101110

Of all the times and seasons and places...*destiny has brought you to me.*

There are no coincidences; there are no chance meetings because your life has already happened, and your days have already been written.

We are living in a time when fear has gripped the hearts and minds of people all over the world.

The evil elite has enacted their plan for a New World Order, and their plan to enslave humanity is no longer a conspiracy theory but a matter of verifiable fact. For those who have studied Agenda 21, the war on small business, personal freedom, personal property ownership, and religious freedom is clearly seen in mainstream media's words, actions, and programming.

Fear is a priceless commodity and is almost as lucrative an industry as racism. *Fear is the weapon of choice* by the elite to not only enslave humanity but to carry out the orders of their Master to *kill, steal, and destroy.*

The truth I am about to share with you has allowed me to live *a life free of fear and anxiety*, where nothing has been impossible for me, and nothing has been out of my grasp. I wake up each day saying, *"God, you've given me another day,"* and I live an amazing, adventurous, and successful life.

Are you living a fearless, anxiety-free, prosperous, and adventurous life?

If so, great!

If not, then continue...

Have you ever traveled on a Train?

Imagine you are riding on a train. If you are riding on a train you are traveling on a track.

If you are traveling on a track, it means that *someone has gone ahead of you to build that track* on which you are traveling.

Someone famous once said, *"And if I go and prepare a place for you, I will come again and receive you to Myself; that where I am, there you may be also."*[1]

If your body is the train, *the vessel in which you are traveling*, then your life is the track on which you are traveling.

---

[1] John 14:3 NKJ Version

1 EINSTEIN AND THE TRAIN

Imagine sitting on a train across from Einstein. You are moving at a certain rate of speed relative to the land around you. Inside the train, you and Einstein are stationary.

Let's now say you get off the train, and Einstein stays on the train, and you see it moving away from you. You are stationary, but relative to you, Einstein inside waving at you, and he is moving at the same speed as the train.

This is the phenomenon of *Relative Motion*.

We see it every day, ***but light behaves in a different way***.

Speed is distance per unit of time.

The speed of light is 186,000 miles per second. The faster you travel; ***the more time slows down***.

In 1905, Einstein developed this theory of Relativity. ***It states that at the speed of light, there is no time.***

2 GOD IS LIGHT

According to the Bible, *"God is light; in him there is no darkness at all."* This is found in the book 1 John chapter 1 verse 5.

If God is light and at the speed of light there is no time, then God is not bound by time, which is why He, *in the person of Jesus,* can raise His head from cross and see you right now at this very moment in the past, while at the same time He can see you from His heavenly throne in the future.

The Sacred Writings in the letter to the Hebrews chapter 13 verse 8 say that *He is the same yesterday, today, and forever.*

In John's book of Revelation chapter 1 verse 8, he writes the words spoken by God about Himself, *"I am the Alpha and the Omega,"* says the Lord God, *"who is, and who was, and who is to come, the Almighty."*

3 YOUR LIFE HAS ALREADY BEEN WRITTEN
1110111 1110010 1101001 1110100 1110100 1100101 1101110

In the book of Psalm chapter 139 verse 16b, King David said to God, *"all the days ordained for me were written in your book before one of them came to be."*

David knew that his life had already been written by the Ancient of Days.

King Solomon, David's son, wrote, *"and the dust returns to the ground it came from, and the spirit returns to God who gave it."* This is found in the book of Ecclesiastes chapter 12 verse 7.

This means that your spirit is immortal.

It was downloaded just as it will one day be uploaded.

In 1901, a physician named Duncan MacDougall once reasoned it should be possible to calculate the weight of a soul by measuring body weight before and after death. He found that *the human body weighs 21 grams less after death*, thus concluding that your *soul or life force or energy* is transferred to somewhere else and weighs approximately 21 grams.[2]

Even an atheist doctor will agree that your spirit or consciousness leaves your body when you die.

It is *"uploaded"* somewhere outside of this reality.

---

[2] MacDougall, Duncan. "Hypothesis Concerning Soul Substance Together with Experimental Evidence of the Existence of Such Substance". American Medicine. New Series Vol 2 (4): 240–43. April 1907.
http://spiritualscientific.com/yahoo_site_admin/assets/docs/MacDougall_article_American_Medicine_Soul_Substance.203123041.pdf

4 EVERYTHING THAT HAS OR WILL HAPPENED IS ALREADY ENCODED IN THE TORAH

1110100 1101111 1110010 1100001 1101000

The Torah, or Jewish Written Law, consists of the five books of the Hebrew Bible – *known more commonly to non-Jews as the "Old Testament"* – that were given by God to Moses on Mount Sinai and included within them, all the biblical laws of Judaism.

Jewish tradition holds that *"Moses received the Torah from Sinai,"* yet there is also an ancient tradition that the Torah existed in Heaven, not only before God revealed it to Moses, but even before the world was created.[3]

The Bible code, *also known as the Torah Code*, is a method described as a *"hidden code"* of selecting Equidistant Letter Sequences from within the 3,300-year-old Hebrew Bible that form words and phrases that demonstrate foreknowledge and prophecy.

The study and results from this cipher have been popularized by Michael Drosnin's book The Bible Code.[4]

---

[3] "Judaism: The Written Law – Torah." Jewish Virtual Library. https://www.jewishvirtuallibrary.org/the-written-law-torah.

[4] See http://torah-codes.net/

The Bible is getting harder to ignore. This timeless document has been the subject of debate for centuries, and now one can just watch the headlines of the world to see that this Book is turning out to be true.

Many Jews believe that everything that has ever happened or will ever happen is found encoded in the Torah.

If the Bible is a credible document to be believed, then it contains ALL human history.

If so, you cannot have the *beginning of all things and the end of all things* in one book without the story of *your life* being in the pages between the beginning and the end.

Archeology is also proving every day that the Bible has always been true. The discoveries of archaeology since the mid-1800s have demonstrated the reliability and plausibility of the Bible narrative.

EBLA ARCHIVE - The discovery of the Ebla archive in northern Syria in the 1970s has shown the Biblical writings concerning the Patriarchs to be viable.

5 STUCK IN THE STORY

When we read about the story of Abraham in the book of Genesis, we are sitting next to God on His throne from His perspective.

We know how Abraham's story ends, *but Abraham is stuck in the story.* Abraham walked in faith, and his faith was verified.

What is faith?

"Now faith is the substance of things hoped for, the evidence of things not seen." (Hebrews 11:1).

God knows the end of your story as well. He knew your story before the foundation of the world. That is why there is the scripture in Proverbs 3:5, *"Trust in the Lord with all your heart and lean not on your own understanding."*

Your life has already happened. Your days have already been written, and you can *put your trust in God*, Who is *"the author and finisher of your faith."*

As the scripture says, *"Looking unto Jesus the author and finisher of our faith; who for the joy that was set before him endured the cross, despising the shame, and is set down at the right hand of the throne of God" (Hebrews 12:2).*

6 THE MATRIX IS TRUE

The Wachowski Brothers, who wrote and directed the movie *The Matrix*, know how right they are when they say that we live in a simulation, but they are not the first to say it.

We are in this simulation, but we are not of this simulation.

It is just as Jesus said in His prayer to the Father about us: *"but they are in the world, and I come to You. Holy Father, keep through Your name those whom You have given Me, that they may be one as We are... I do not pray that You should take them out of the world, but they You should keep them from the evil one. They are not of the world, just as I am not of the world." (John 17:11b; 15-16).*

Elon Musk has also supported this simulation theory as well when he said, *"If you assume any rate of improvement at all, games will eventually be indistinguishable from reality,"* Musk said before concluding, *"We're most likely in a simulation."*[5]

---

[5] Powell, Corey S. "Elon Musk says we may live in a simulation. Here's how we might tell if he's right." NBC News. October 3, 2018, https://www.nbcnews.com/mach/science/what-simulation-hypothesis-why-some-think-life-simulated-reality-ncna913926.

Astrophysicist Neil deGrasse Tyson agrees, giving *"better than 50-50 odds"* that the simulation hypothesis is correct.

They weren't the first to say it either.

7 THE SECRET TO DÉJÀ VU

1100100 1100101 1101010 1100001 100000 1110110 1110101

"Have you ever had a dream, Neo, that you were so sure was real? What if you were unable to wake from that dream? How would you know the difference between the dream world and the real world?" - Morpheus to Neo in The Matrix. [6]

You've had it happen to you before. *Deja Vu.*

You could swear that what you were experiencing had not only happened before, but sometimes you were able to predict what was about to happen next.

According to Wikipedia: Déjà vu French: "already seen" is a French loanword expressing when you have done something, and you experience the same feelings or the feeling that one has lived through the present situation before.

What would you think if I told you that you *HAVE* seen it before because your life has already happened and the *"you"* that is beyond time is connecting to the *"you"* who is still stuck in your story, on your track of time, walking out your destiny as if to say, *"Just walk this out. Have no*

---

[6] *The Matrix*. Directed by the Wachowskis, performances by Laurence Fishburne and Keane Reeves, Warner Bro, March 1999.

fear. It has already happened, and everything will be ok."?

I believe the *"already seen"* is a reality beyond your regular perception.

8 YOUR PERCEPTION IS YOUR REALITY

1110010 1100101 1100001 1101100 1101001 1110100 1111001

In The Matrix, after Neo had taken the Red Pill and had been extracted from the realm of the system, he complained to Morpheus that his eyes were hurting. Morpheus' reply was, *"That is because you have never used them before."*

Perception was once Neo's reality.

In the early 2000s, I was an adjunct professor teaching Intro to Philosophy at Tulsa Community College when we came to the section of Metaphysics, which is the study of reality.

Plato, the pupil of the Great Philosopher Socrates, wrote an allegory called *"The Cave"*, *The Allegory of the Cave can be found in Book VII of Plato's best-known work, "The Republic,"* a lengthy dialogue on the nature of justice, according to Indiana Wesleyan University.[7]

In *"The Cave,"* men were chained, hands, heads, and feet inside a cave facing a cave wall.

---

[7] See
https://www.indwes.edu/academics/jwhc/_files/Plato_s%20Allegory%20of%20the%20Cave.pdf#:~:text=The%20Allegory%20of%20the%20Cave%20can%20be%20found,discussion%20of%20the%20education%20required%20of%20a%20Philosopher-King.

Because of these chains, they were not able to move their heads around to look anywhere else but straight ahead towards the wall of the cave.

Behind them, there was a fire, and their only perception of reality was shadows of objects cast upon the cave wall because of the fire and the people contributing to the illusion.

One of these prisoners was released from his chains and was allowed to climb out of the cave to witness the wonders of the true reality. He saw the actual people, animals, and places in wondrous color and amazing detail - an amazing world he could barely describe. Then he saw the sun in all its beauty, bathing all creation in its life-giving light.

When he returned to share the truth of this wondrous reality with the other prisoners, *they laughed at him and sought to kill him.*

Plato knew that perception was reality.

That the average person who vicariously walks through this life doing what they are told to do, thinking what they are told to think, and believe what they are told to believe, would rather live a convenient lie than to know the inconvenient truth.

Plato knew human nature in that people, or shall I say sheeple do what works for them *until it no longer works for them*, good or bad, happy or sad, righteous or evil.

9 WHAT YOU CAN TOLERATE, YOU WILL NEVER CHANGE

1110100 1101111 1101100 1100101 1110010 1100001 1110100 1100101

The reason so many women live with abusive husbands, or why so many men live with domineering, abusive wives, *is because they know how to function in an abusive situation*.

They would rather function in dysfunction than face the fear of the unknown, even if the unknown is a new adventure leading to a peaceful and happy life.

Settling for the hell you know instead of awakening to truth and taking action to change your stars is the way of the world – *the way of sheep destined for the slaughter.*

What you can tolerate, you will never change.

This is why I tell people that *I would rather die than live a mediocre life!*

Don't settle for anything - a bad job, a bad marriage, one-sided relationships, or a mediocre life.

Break your chains, my friend, and leave the cave once and for all!

10 THE RED PILL PROPHET

1110010 1100101 1100100 100000 1110000 1101001 1101100 1101100

"You take the blue pill, the story ends, you wake up in your bed and believe whatever you want to believe. You take the red pill, you stay in wonderland, and I show you how deep the rabbit hole goes...all I am offering you is the truth - nothing more." -Morpheus in The Matrix

Pontius Pilate once asked Jesus, *"What is Truth?"* This is found in the Bible in the book of John 18:37-38, *"You are a king, then!"* said Pilate.

Jesus answered, *"You say that I am a king. In fact, the reason I was born and came into the world is to testify to the truth. Everyone on the side of truth listens to me."*

In the movie, *The Matrix*, the character Neo was "The Chosen One," who was to re-emerge into the simulation to destroy the work of the evil one set the captives free.

In this sense, *Jesus was the real-life "Red Pill Prophet."*

11 JESUS IS HISTORY

Every year *Time Magazine* comes out with the same lame article asking, *"Was Jesus a Real Person?"*

They know He was.

Even the Roman Senate Annals in the Vatican verify that not only was Jesus real but that most of His miracles were witnessed and recorded by the Romans themselves.

This Messiah can be seen in history and His influences woven into world history from Genesis to Revelation, *from the beginning of history to its end.*

Even Napoleon had this to say about Jesus, "I marvel that whereas the ambitious dreams of myself, Caesar, and Alexander should have vanished into thin air, a Judean peasant-Jesus should be able to stretch His hands across the centuries and control the destinies of men and nations."[8]

---

[8] Petton, Dr. Larry. "Quotes From Napoleon on Jesus". Sermoncentral.com. March 8, 2016. https://www.sermoncentral.com/sermon-illustrations/84136/quotes-from-napoleon-on-jesus-by-dr-larry-petton

C.S. Lewis, one of the most iconic authors in human history, had this to say about Jesus, "I am trying here to prevent anyone saying the really foolish thing that people often say about Him *[that is, Christ]:* 'I'm ready to accept Jesus as a great moral teacher, but I don't accept His claim to be God.' That is the one thing we must not say. A man who was merely a man and said the sort of things Jesus said would not be a great moral teacher. He would either be a lunatic-on a level with the man who says he is a poached egg-or else he would be the Devil of Hell. ***You must make your choice.*** Either this man was, and is, the Son of God: or else a madman or something worse...You can shut Him up for a fool, you can spit at Him and kill Him as a demon; or ***you can fall at His feet and call Him Lord and God.*** But let us not come up with any patronizing nonsense about His being a great human teacher. He has not left that open to us. He did not intend to."[9]

---

[9] From *"Mere Christianity"* by C.S. Lewis.

12 JIM MORRISON, "THE DOORS" AND JESUS
1100100 1101111 1101111 1110010 1110011

Jim Morrison of The Doors was a genius with an IQ of 149. He considered himself a Shaman and more of a poet than a singer.

He claimed that as a little boy, he came across a gruesome car accident of male workers in which the spirit of a dead man, *a Native American man*, entered his body and determined the course of his life.

This self-proclaimed "Lizard King" named his band "The Doors" as a reference to doors into the ultimate reality.

In 2010, the quotation website *Thinkexist* credited Jim Morrison with the following, *"There are things known and things unknown, and in between are the Doors."*[10]

 While Morrison's life was once saved by Nuns, we have no record of him being saved by Jesus.

According to the socurrent.com website, during The Doors 1968 European tour, Morrison didn't actually take the stage. Instead, he was given a powerful bit of hash by Bob Hite, singer for Canned Heat, which rendered him unconscious. He was found by a group of nuns and taken to the

---

[10] See

http://en.thinkexist.com/search/searchquotation.asp?search=There+are+things+known+and+things +unknown%2C+And+in+between+are+the+Doors

hospital, where he recovered."[11]

Morrison was sort of a self-proclaimed prophet "showing the way" to the world, but in the end, he was not able to save himself. He is known as being a member of "The 27 Club," where so many rock stars have died at the age of 27.

One may say that the Prince of Darkness has granted fame and riches to many in the entertainment world, but in the end, they were merely sheep destined for slaughter.

If only Jim had come across the Red Pill Prophet, who said in *John 10:7-10 (ESV)*, *"Truly, truly, I say to you, I am the door of the sheep. All who came before me are thieves and robbers, but the sheep did not listen to them. I am the door. If anyone enters by me, he will be saved and will go in and out and find pasture. The thief comes only to steal and kill and destroy. I came that they may have life and have it abundantly."*

Jesus is the door to the ultimate reality, and your life was written in His book before time began.

---

[11] Leger, Eva. "Jim Morrison: 15 Interesting Facts You Didn't Know: Number Eight: He Was Rescued by Nuns." Socurrent.com. https://socurrent.com/jim-morrison-15-interesting-facts-you-didnt-know/

13 A REQUEST TO PRAY
1110000 1110010 1100001 1111001

I remember getting a phone call from a person whom I had spoken into their life, that they would speak before leaders.

He said, *"Brant, I'm speaking in front of 1,000 people tonight, and could really use your prayers."*

I replied, *"I'll pray - but it has already happened exactly the way God has ordained it."*

If you come to this truth of your life being written, *you can trust God that things will happen exactly the way they are supposed to.*

As Bobby McFerrin wrote in his hit; "Don't Worry, Be Happy." According to Wikipedia; ""Don't Worry, Be Happy" is a song by American musician Bobby McFerrin released in 1988. It was the first a cappella song to reach number-one on the Billboard Hot 100 chart, a position it held for two weeks. Originally released in conjunction with the film Cocktail, the song peaked at No. 1 on September 24, 1988, displacing "Sweet Child o' Mine" by Guns N' Roses."[12]

---

[12] See https://en.wikipedia.org/wiki/Don%27t_Worry,_Be_Happy

Jesus said in the book of Matthew 6:34, *"Therefore do not worry about tomorrow, for tomorrow will worry about itself. Each day has enough trouble of its own."* Jesus also said that you cannot add one hour to your life by worrying, *so why worry? (Luke 12:25-26).*

14 HE'S GOT THE WHOLE WORLD IN HIS HANDS

1101000 1101001 1110011 100000 1101000 1100001 1101110 1100100 1110011

Remember that old song that some of us sang as children, *"He's Got the Whole World in His Hands"*?

You have heard some people say, *"God's got this!"* or *"Just give it to God."*

I used to think that statement was such a ridiculous statement until I lived longer and have seen in my own life that **God is truly in control.**

The Bible says that He laughs at the nations. He sets up leaders and takes them down as His will.[13]

The Bible says that *"God works for the good of those who love him, who have been called according to his purpose" (Romans 8:28).*

Have you ever looked back on your life and seen how God, in His brilliance, was able to take a bad situation and turn it into *a masterpiece?*

God had already written your days in His book before you were born.

---

[13] Psalm 2:4

You don't have the power to bum God out or throw God off His game!

Cast your cares on Him, *for He cares for you! (Psalm 55:22).*

30

15 THE GREAT CLOUD OF WITNESSES

1101000 1101001 1110011 100000 1101000 1100001 1101110 1100100 110111
1101001 1110100 1101110 1100101 1110011 1110011 1100101 1110011

"Therefore, since we are surrounded by such a great cloud of witnesses, let us throw off everything that hinders and the sin that so easily entangles. And let us run with perseverance the race marked out for us" (Hebrews 12:1).

A Great Cloud of Witnesses. It is taken from the Greek word *nephos*. It describes clouds — *just like the clouds you see in the sky*.

Our lives are being witnessed by watchers.

We are in a simulation where everything is observed and recorded.

Revelation 20:12 says, *"And I saw the dead, small and great, standing before God, and books were opened. And another book was opened, which is the Book of Life. The dead were judged according to their works, by the things which were written in the books."*

Your life has already been written in God's book before you were born.

God knows your strengths and your weaknesses.
He knows the nature of man.

He knows that man would need *a savior*.

He made a way for us to overcome this simulation before time began.

He sees you, *and the battle is already won*.

The Word says we *are seated with Christ in heavenly places* far above all powers and principalities of this world.

That means we can live above our circumstances because we fight from a place of victory. *"And God raised us up together, and made us sit together in heavenly places in Christ Jesus" (Ephesians 2:6).*

If the Bible is true, *and it is*, if our lives have already been written, and they are, and if we are seated with Christ in heavenly realms right now...*THEN YOU ARE WATCHING YOURSELF RIGHT NOW LEARNING THIS TRUTH.*

Your life has already happened.

Your days were already written, and you are among the great cloud of witnesses watching history unfold. The *you* outside of time is calling to the you stuck in the story, and the message is clear, *just keep walking towards God.*

Trust Him with all your heart, mind, soul, and strength.

Live fearlessly!

16 TRUST IN GOD ALLOWS ME TO LIVE FEARLESSLY AND WITHOUT ANXIETY

1100110 1100101 1100001 1110010 1101100 1100101 1110011 1110011

I've been on vacation for years. My life has already been written, and I know that God will work out everything to my good.

Jesus said that a person cannot add one hour to their life by worrying. He said to let tomorrow worry about itself. ***This is living in the now.***

I am not fearful of anything or anyone.

I am free from the opinions of people who don't even know who they are.

Every day I awaken, I say, ***"God, you've given me another day."***

I get a thought, I make a call, and it becomes!

I live my life as if it has already happened.

Any decision that is not in line with who I want to be, I simply decide not to do it!

I have ultimate freedom, and nothing is impossible for me.

At the end of the day, I ask myself if I did my best before I go to bed. If that answer is no, then I do what I can before my head hits the pillow in good conscience.

17 TRUSTING IN GOD DOESN'T ALWAYS MEAN AGREEING WITH GOD

1110100 1110010 1110101 1110011 1110100 1101001 1101110 1100111

God's ways are not our ways, and He says that to us; *"For my thoughts are not your thoughts, neither are your ways my ways,' declares the Lord. 'As the heavens are higher than the earth, so are my ways higher than your ways and my thoughts than your thoughts'"* (Isaiah 55:8-9).

That's His disclaimer.

I don't always agree with how God does things, *and that's ok.*

King David didn't always agree with God. Much of the book of Psalms is filled with David tweeting how angry he is with how things are going and how God is handling it, and that is perfectly fine. We aren't commanded to agree with God. *We only have to trust Him.*

I will never forget seeing happenings in my life where I stopped and said, *"God, I don't agree with You on this. This isn't how I would handle it, but I trust You. I will trust You!"*

I had come to the conclusion that *God will use whom He wants, how*

"

He wants when He wants, and how He wants because He is God and I am not!"

This was a relief to realize that God's ways are not my ways, and all I have to do is trust Him. He has already written my life in the pages of His book, and my life has already happened!

18 MOST OF WHAT HAPPENS TO YOU IS NOT GOD OR THE DEVIL

1101001 1110100 100111 1110011 100000 1111001 1101111 1110101

My life changed when I quit blaming God for bad things that happened in my life.

I remember the day I "Let God off the hook". I realized that *I had become an opponent of God in my anger and pride*.

"God opposes the proud but shows favor to the humble" (James 4:6).

I stopped the world, owned where I was, and said, *"God, please forgive me for blaming You for bad things that have happened in my life."*

I know He forgave me.

As surely as I am writing to you, I heard in my heart, *"Brant, most of what happens to you has nothing to do with Me and nothing to do with Satan but because of your own decisions. You didn't ask me before you married the first time. I wasn't in your first marriage. but I blessed it,"* and He went on to other decisions saying the same thing; *"I wasn't in this, I wasn't in that, but I blessed it!"*

This truth set me free. It set me on the road to making better decisions in the future.

19 WHAT DOES GOD WANT AND WHAT IS GOD'S WILL FOR MY LIFE?

1101101 1111001 100000 1101100 1101001 1100110 1100101

The Bible is clear about what God wants. God wants no man to perish but for all men to come to the knowledge of the truth.

"This is good, and pleases God our Savior, who wants all people to be saved and to come to a knowledge of the truth" (1 Timothy 2:3-4).

That's His will, for no man to perish, but for every man to come to the knowledge of the truth.

I have often said in crowds and on the airwaves that I know God's will for your life. People usually respond as if I'm some type of fortune teller, and I laugh and smile at their usual response in saying, *"No, but listen to me. God's will is for no man to perish but for every man to come to the knowledge of the truth. Hold out your hand and ask yourself, "What has God put into your hands: your dreams, your passions, your successes, your tragedies, your life experience – what has He put into your hand to help HIM accomplish His will for no man to perish but for every man to come to the knowledge of the truth? THAT is HIS will for your life! For some of you, it may be teaching. It may be singing, writing, painting, speaking, or making money for good causes for some of you. It is really that simple."*

20 GOD CHOSE YOU

1100111 1101111 1100100 100000 1100011 1101000 1101111 1110011
1100101 100000 1111001 1101111 1110101

In the movie The Matrix, Morpheus knew Neo from his birth and had followed him his entire life until the moment was right to engage him.

In the same way, *God is engaging you right at this moment*.

He knew you before you were born.

Psalm 139:16 says, *"Your eyes saw my unformed body; all the days ordained for me were written in your book before one of them came to be."*

You were fearfully and wonderfully made.[14] *You were no accident.*

Remember, there are no accidents or coincidences.

Ephesians 1:4 (NLT) says, *"Even before he made the world, God loved us and chose us in Christ to be holy and without fault in His eyes."*

Ephesians 1:4, (CSB) says it this way, *"For he chose us in Him, before the foundation of the world, to be holy and blameless in love before Him."*

---

[14] Psalm 139:14

"

20 JESUS SAVED YOU BEFORE THE BEGINNING OF THIS SIMULATION

1001010 1100101 1110011 1110101 1110011 100000 1110011 1100001
1110110 1100101 1110011

2 Timothy 1:9 says, *"He has saved us and called us to a holy life—not because of anything we have done but because of His own purpose and grace. This grace was given us in Christ Jesus before the beginning of time."*

Romans 5:8 says, "But God demonstrates *His own love for us* in this: While we were still sinners, *Christ died for us.*"

In The Matrix Trilogy, Neo gives his life for the lives of all humanity. Ironically, Neo is laid out like Jesus on the cross. This concept is nothing new.

Hebrews 10:10 says, *"And by that will, we have been made holy through the sacrifice of the body of Jesus Christ once for all."*

God has known you before the beginning of time.

Your spirit came from Him, and He knew you, released your soul into this simulation to give you a chance to find Him and choose Him, or to live your life as a slave to a system that poisons your food, air, and water, sells you cancer treatments and taxes your family when you die.

44

21 YOUR DESTINY WAS NOT TO BE A VICTIM OF THIS CULTURE

1100100 1100101 1110011 1110100 1101001 1101110 1111001

It has been said that a victim of this culture is out of shape, addicted, in debt with a house full of junk.

You were *not* destined to live a life as a slave to this culture.

You were destined to live a life of greatness and a life of contribution to humanity.

You were destined to celebrate the creation of your being, in loving your fellow man and making this world a better place.

Notice the anger of those who choose to live as slaves towards those of us who refuse to live a mediocre life!

Stop the world. Own where you are.

Blame nobody.

Forgive everyone.

Forgive yourself for settling for a mediocre life.

Stand up! Encourage yourself with a spirit of gratefulness, worship, and the hounds of hell that encircle you will run away, for they cannot exist in the *atmosphere of gratefulness.*

22 LUCIFER AND THE BARN

1110100 1101000 1100101 100000 1100010 1100001 1110010 1101110

There is an old legend of a man who met the devil in a barn.

Lucifer was sitting on a pile of seeds when the man asked, *"What are those?"*

Lucifer replied, *"These are the seeds of discouragement. I plant them all over the world, but there is one place where they will not take, and that is in the heart of a grateful man."*

Be encouraged!

Count your blessings.

Thank God for His goodness with a heart of gratefulness and blow the shofar of victory and not the shofar of fear!

23 FEAR IS THE CURRENCY OF EVIL

1101110 1101111 100000 1100110 1100101 1100001 1110010

Fear is a lucrative commodity used by the elite and their media to control you, kill you, steal your joy, and end your life. *Period.*

This global genocide in the form of a bioweapon disguised as a pandemic where hospitals receive bonuses for your death; is evidence enough that evil forces rule this world for a time, *but God has given you a way to beat this evil system.*

He has given you the **Red Pill** to awaken to the true reality and to live a life free of fear!

The Native Americans would not allow fear into their camps. When their warriors would return from battle, they would walk between the elders of the tribe, and if anger, hate, or fear was detected, they were told to go to *"the sacred place"* to get clean and free from fear. Then they would be allowed to come back into the assembly of the people.

Rid yourself of fear by going to the sacred place of forgiveness and gratefulness towards others and God.

24 YOU WERE NOT BORN TO LIVE IN FEAR - GOD HAS NOT GIVEN US A SPIRIT OF FEAR

1101110 1101111 100000 1100110 1100101 1100001 1110010

2 Timothy 1:7 says (NLT), *"God has not given us a spirit of fear and timidity, but of power, love, and self-discipline."* Some translations say, *"a sound mind."*

A sound mind means a mind capable of good, positive, and free-thinking.

What would the world do with a person free of fear or anxiety where nothing is impossible for those who believe?

What would your life look like if you were fearless and free from worry or anxiety?

How free would you be *if you forgave everyone and forgave yourself?*

25 THE RED PILL PROPHET CALLS OUT TO YOU NOW

Jesus said in John 11:25, *"I am the resurrection and the life. The one who believes in me will live, even though they die."*

Jesus also says in John 14:6, *"I am the way and the truth and the life. No one comes to the Father except through me."*

It is written in the Bible that *"Everyone who calls on the name of the Lord will be saved"* (Romans 10:13).

God says in Jeremiah 33:3, *"Call to me and I will answer you and tell you great and unsearchable things you do not know."*

Now that is the ultimate Red Pill.

There are no accidents. There are no coincidences. There are no such things.

Your life has already been written. Your life has already happened.

The Red Pill Prophet is Jesus, and He has come to set you free. Be free to live a life of fearlessness. A life without anxiety. A life where nothing is out of your grasp because you know this is not your home.

Drink life. *Follow the Red Pill Prophet!*

Now go and awaken the others to the freedom you now enjoy!

Jesus said in John 8:36, *"So if the Son sets you free, you will be free indeed."*

You were not born to be a slave in the prison of your mind. *"It is for freedom that Christ has set us free. Stand firm, then, and do not let yourselves be burdened again by a yoke of slavery"* (Galatians 5:1).

Free your mind.

Cast off your chains of fear, doubt, and anxiety, and in the words of Morpheus, *"Welcome to the Real World."*

PLATO – THE ALLEGORY OF THE CAVE

(*Republic*, Book Seven)
Translated by Oleg Bychkov, Theology Department, St. Bonaventure University

SOCRATES: At this point I will show you something about the nature of education and ignorance. Picture the following in your mind. Imagine human beings living in an underground cave-like residence. Its entrance opens up to the light and reaches all along the cave. They have been there since their childhood, their ankles and necks chained, unable to move or turn their heads, forced to look ahead. The light from a fire blazing at a distance comes from above and behind them. Between the fire and the prisoners there is a raised walkway. Imagine also a low wall built along the way, similar to the screen that divides puppeteers from the audience and allows them to show puppets over it.

GLAUCON: I picture the scene.

SOCRATES: Now imagine that people walk behind the wall and carry various artifacts that extend above the wall. These artifacts include carvings of humans and other animals made of stone, wood, and other materials. Some of the people carrying these object are talking, while others are silent.

GLAUCON: You paint a strange picture and describe strange prisoners.

SOCRATES: They are like ourselves. Now do you think they see anything else except their own shadows, or the shadows of one another, which light from the fire casts on to the opposite wall of the cave?

GLAUCON: How could they see anything else if they were forced to keep their heads still for their whole life?

SOCRATES: And what would they see of the objects that are being carried? Would they not see only shadows of them as well?

GLAUCON: What else?

SOCRATES: And if they were able to talk to one another, would they not think that the object of their conversation were the shadows they saw in front of them?

GLAUCON: Absolutely.

SOCRATES: And what if an echo bounced off the opposite wall of the prison? Would they not think that when one of the passers-by spoke the voice came from the passing shadow?

GLAUCON: Definitely.

SOCRATES: Such prisoners would think that the truth is nothing but the shadows cast by the artifacts.

GLAUCON: Most certainly.

SOCRATES: Now imagine what would happen naturally if the prisoners were released from their shackles and cured of their ignorance. Right after they are released and suddenly forced to stand up, turn their necks around, walk, and look towards the light, these activities will cause them pain; because of the bright glare they would be unable to see those things which they previously had seen only as shadows. Now what do you think they would say if one were to tell them that what they saw before was fooling them, but that now, when they are closer to what really exists and when they face that which more truly exists, they see more clearly, in a straightforward manner? What if that person pointed to the objects as they passed and asked the former prisoners to tell him what they were? Don't you think they would be baffled and think that the shadows they formerly saw were truer than the objects that are now being pointed out to them?

GLAUCON: Far truer.

SOCRATES: And if they were forced to look straight at the light, would that not make their eyes hurt? Would they not try to avoid the light and turn back to the things that they can see? And would they not think that in reality the shadows are more clear than the objects they are forced to look at?

GLAUCON: True.

SOCRATES: But what if someone dragged them along a steep and harsh ascent against their will, and did not let go until they were dragged right into the sunlight? Would they not feel pain and discomfort? And if they walked towards the sun and their eyes suddenly filled with brilliant light, would they be able to see even one of those things that are now called true realities?

GLAUCON: No, not right away.

SOCRATES: I think that if they wanted to see the objects of the upper world they would need to grow accustomed to them. First of all, it will be easier for them to see the shadows. After that, they will see the reflections of people and other things in the water, and only after that they will see the objects themselves. After that, they will see celestial objects and the sky itself; it will be easier to see them first at night, by looking at the stars and the light of the moon, than during the day, by looking at the sun or the light of the sun.

GLAUCON: How could it be otherwise?

SOCRATES: Last of all, I think, they will be able to see the sun, and not mere reflections of it in the water or other media. They will be able to look at the sun itself directly and see it as it is.

GLAUCON: Definitely.

SOCRATES: Now after making all these observations they will conclude that it is the sun that is responsible for the four seasons and the passing of the years, and that it governs all that exists in the visible world, and that in some way the sun was even the cause of all those things that they used to see in the cave.

GLAUCON: Clearly, they will come to such conclusions after having made those observations.

SOCRATES: What do you think, then? When they recall where they used to live, and the backward wisdom of that place, and the fellow prisoners they once had, would they not think that this change is fortunate for them, and then would they not pity those who stayed behind?

GLAUCON: No question.

SOCRATES: What if some honors, praise, and gifts were bestowed on them by other cave dwellers while they still were in the cave for their superior ability to detect the passing shadows; to remember best in which sequence those shadows usually moved (which of them went before, and which followed after, and which moved together); and to predict how the shadows would move in the future based on their past observations? Do you think they would care for such honors or even envy the ones who were honored and considered powerful among the cave dwellers? Or do you think they would rather choose "to become servants of a poor man," to quote Homer (Odyssey 11.489-490), and to endure anything, rather than admire such things and live in that way?

GLAUCON: Yes, I think that they would rather suffer anything than accept this sort of life.

SOCRATES: Now imagine this. If such a person goes back down into the cave and ends up back in the same boat as the other prisoners, would her eyes not be filled with darkness after she suddenly comes out of the sun?

GLAUCON: To be sure.

SOCRATES: And what would happen if such a person were once again to compete against the permanent cave dwellers in judging those shadows? Remember that his sight would still be weak before his eyes once again got used to the darkness, and the recovery time could be considerable. Would he not, then, become the butt of jokes, and would they not say about him that up he went and down he came with his eyes totally destroyed, and that it is not advisable even to think of climbing up? And if someone attempted to free another prisoner and then lead him upwards, would they not kill that leader if they could only lay their hands on him?

GLAUCON: No doubt.

SOCRATES: Now, dear Glaucon, apply this entire imaginary picture to our previous discussion. The prison-house stands for the visible world; the light of the fire in the cave represents the power of the sun. And you will not miss my intended meaning if you interpret the journey upwards (and the sight of the things that are up above) as the ascent of the soul into the intelligible world, for this is what you wish to hear about. Only God knows if my attempt has been successful, but here is how things seem to me.

In the world of knowledge, the idea of good appears last of all and we are barely capable of seeing it. However, when we do manage to see it, we conclude that it is the cause of all that is beautiful and right. It gives birth to light and to the lord of light in the visible world, and in the intelligible world it rules itself and is the source of truth and intelligibility. Now anyone who intends to act prudently either in public or private life must have her mind's eye fixed upon this idea.

GLAUCON: I think I follow you, as far as I can.

SOCRATES: Come, now, and follow me a step farther. You should not be surprised that those who come to this place have no desire to be involved in the affairs of the cave dwellers. Instead, their souls long to remain here forever. This is how they are likely to behave, since that is what our analogy so far has suggested.

GLAUCON: Yes, very likely.

SOCRATES: Now consider the following. Suppose someone comes down from contemplating divine things to participate in human affairs. (Remember that such a person's sight would still be weak before he gets adjusted sufficiently to the surrounding darkness.) Now suppose that before his eyes get used to the darkness he is compelled to fight in courts of law, or in other places, about the shadows of justice as opposed to the objects of which these are the shadows. Suppose that he will have to struggle to understand how these things are perceived by those who have never seen justice itself. Do you think it is surprising if he badly discredits himself and then appears totally ridiculous?

GLAUCON: Not for a moment.

SOCRATES: However, anyone who has common sense would recall that someone's vision can be impaired for two reasons. The first is when someone comes out of the light and goes into the dark, and the second is when one comes out of the dark and goes into the light. Now assuming that the mind's eye works in the same way, when a sensible person sees a soul whose vision is confused and impaired, he would not burst into laughter senselessly. He would first try to determine whether this soul's vision is impaired because it is unaccustomed to the dark on its way from the world of light, or it is dazzled by bright glare on its way out of the life of ignorance and to the world of light. Now after a sensible person has determined this, he would consider the life and condition of former kind fortunate, and would pity the latter kind. And if he chose to laugh at the latter person, it would make more sense than to laugh at the former person, who is on her way from the upper world.

GLAUCON: What you say is very reasonable.

SOCRATES: Now if this is correct, our way of thinking about these things should be as follows. We must not think that education really works the way some self-professed educators say it works. For they say that knowledge is not present in the soul and that they somehow put it in there, like sight into blind eyes.

GLAUCON: This is exactly what they say.

SOCRATES: However, our present discussion here indicates that this capacity, as well as the instrument that allows us to learn, exists in everyone's soul already. It is as if our eyes were unable to turn from darkness to light without the entire body; in the same way, our instrument of learning, together with the entire soul, must keep turning away from the fleeting appearances of things, until our soul is able to see steadily into the true nature of things and detect the clearest part of it, which we call the good. Is this not true?

GLAUCON: It is.

SOCRATES: So there should be some art of turning around that would consist in finding the easiest and most efficient way of turning to light. This is not the art that gives us the ability to see, because we already have that; instead, it enables us to turn in the right direction and look where we are supposed to. Should there not be such an art?

GLAUCON: Most likely.

SOCRATES: Now the other so-called virtues of the soul come closer to the fine qualities of the body, for even when they are not initially present, they can be developed later by habit and exercise. But it seems that the virtue of wisdom more than anything else is akin to something divine, for it never loses its power, except that this turning around can turn it either into something useful and valuable or into something useless and harmful. Have you never observed a clever crook—how sharp his sight is and how keenly his narrow mind sees the things to which it turns? His eyesight is by no means impaired, but it is forced to serve evil purposes, and the more sharply he sees, the more evil his deeds are.

GLAUCON: Very true.

SOCRATES: But what if the instrument of sight attached to such natures were to be trimmed down in their childhood and severed from, as it were, the leaden weights that have been tied to it from birth? For those weights gravitate towards gluttony and other such sensual pleasures and desires and deflect the vision of these souls downwards. What if their instrument of sight were freed from these weights and turned in the opposite direction to face true realities? Would that same instrument in those same people not see those realities as sharply as they currently see what their eyes are turned to now?

GLAUCON: Most likely.

SOCRATES: But what about the following? Would the following not be likely, or rather certain from what has been said? Consider two categories of people. The first are the uneducated and ignorant of the truth. The others are those who are allowed to remain permanently in training. Neither category can ever become able administrators of the state. Not the former, because they have no single goal in their life, and one must have some end in sight while doing everything that they do, either privately or publicly. Not the latter, because they will not do anything on their own accord, thinking that they are already living far away in the islands of the blessed.

GLAUCON: Very true.

SOCRATES: In that case, then, if we were the founders of the state, our task would be to compel the best minds to attain that learning which we have previously shown to be the greatest of all, that is, to see the good after they have completed their climb up to the higher regions. However, once they have seen enough upon their ascent, our further task is not to permit them what they are currently allowed to do.

GLAUCON: And what is that?

SOCRATES: Why, of course, not to permit them to remain in the upper regions and to refuse to go back down to the prisoners and to participate in their labors and honors, whether they are serious or worthless.

GLAUCON: But would we not do them wrong by making their life worse while it is possible for them to live better?

SOCRATES: You don't seem to realize, my friend, that the law is not concerned with the well-being of any one class of people in the state by giving them a special status; its aim is the well-being of the entire state. One achieves this aim by holding the citizens together by persuasion or compulsion and by making sure they serve the common good and benefit others as much as they can. For these purposes, qualified people are installed throughout the state not so that they could do whatever they want to, but to ensure the cohesion of the state through them.

GLAUCON: True, I haven't thought of that.

SOCRATES: See, Glaucon, we will not do wrong by those lovers of wisdom among us if we compel them to care for others and protect them, but we will ask them to do the right thing. For we will tell them: "Those who become lovers of wisdom in other states usually do not participate in their political activities. They grow up on their own, for none of the political systems want to have anything to do with them. It is also fair that someone who matures on her own and does not owe anybody for her upbringing does not have to provide upbringing and nurture to anybody. However, we have made you, as it were, to be queens of the hive, leaders of yourselves and of the rest of the citizens, and we have educated you much better and more perfectly than the rest and made you more able to bear this double responsibility. Now each of you must take turns, go down into the cave where the others live and get accustomed to seeing in the dark. For once you do get accustomed to the conditions of the cave you will be able to see a thousand times better than the cave dwellers and will know what all the shadows are and what casts them, for you have seen true beauty, true justice, and true goodness. And in this way the state, both for your sake and for our sake, will be governed by people who are truly aware of reality, and not by those who wander in the land of dreams, like in the other states that are currently governed by those who fight each other about shadows and struggle for power as if it were some great good. But in truth the situation is as follows: the state is necessarily governed in the best and most peaceful manner if those who are destined to rule it are the ones most reluctant to rule, and the state where the rulers are most eager to rule fares the worst."

GLAUCON: Quite so.

SOCRATES: What do you think, then? Upon hearing this, will our nurslings refuse to obey us and will they remain unwilling to take part in the daily labors of the state, taking their turns, while spending most of their time with one another without getting their hands dirty?

GLAUCON: Impossible. For we will ask something fair of the people who have a sense of fairness. It is most certain that every one of them will feel obligated to take power, which is the opposite of what is the case with rulers of currently existing states.

SOCRATES: So this is how things stand, my friend. If you will design a life for intended rulers that is better than the life of a mere ruler, you will be able to have a well-managed state. For only in such a state will those rule who are truly rich, not in gold but in virtue and wisdom, the sort of things that a truly blessed person should be rich in. However, if those who crave only after their own private advantage take on the administration of public affairs, thinking that this is how they grab at the greatest good, the state will never be managed well. A struggle for power will result, and this internal domestic war will destroy both themselves and the rest of the state.

GLAUCON: Most true.

SOCRATES: The life that embodies the true love of wisdom, then, is the only life that looks down upon political power. Or can you think of any other?

GLAUCON: By Zeus, I cannot.

ABOUT THE AUTHOR

BRANT FRICKER is an international media producer and television personality. Nicknamed, "Dream Maker" in the early 90's, Brant has been living out his dreams for decades now, and his passion has been to help individuals step into their own dreams. Having achieved marketing and music success early in life, Brant's success skyrocketed when he had a revelation about God and time. This new life of fearlessness free of anxiety has empowered Brant to express more success since this revelation than his entire marketing, music and ministry career since 1983.

www.ingramcontent.com/pod-product-compliance
Lightning Source LLC
Chambersburg PA
CBHW061625130726
47996CB00003B/1128